BRAIN GAMES®

FIND THE CAT

pil

Publications International, Ltd.

Cover and interior art: Shutterstock.com

Puzzle illustrators: Ashley Joyce, Nick LaShure

Brain Games is a registered trademark of Publications International, Ltd.

Louis Weber, CEO
Publications International, Ltd.
8140 Lehigh Avenue
Morton Grove, IL 60053

Permission is never granted for commercial purposes.

ISBN: 978-1-64030-457-4

Manufactured in China.

8 7 6 5 4 3 2 1

Welcome to *Brain Games®: Find the Cat!* Real cats can get into cabinets or sneak out through an open window, but no matter the setting, you'll find one hidden cat in each photo in this book. It's fun to search for a friendly furry familiar, and it's good for your brain: research suggests a varied routine of regular mental exercise can help keep your brain feeling and acting healthier. If you get stumped, check the answers in the back.

Answer on page 133.

Answer on page 133.

Answer on page 133.

Answer on page 133.

Answer on page 134.

Answer on page 134.

Answer on page 134.

wer on page 135.

Answer on page 135.

Answer on page 135.

Answer on page 135.

Answer on page 136.

Answer on page 136

Answer on page 136.

19

Answer on page 136.

Answer on page 137.

Answer on page 137.

Answer on page 137.

Answer on page 137.

Answer on page 138.

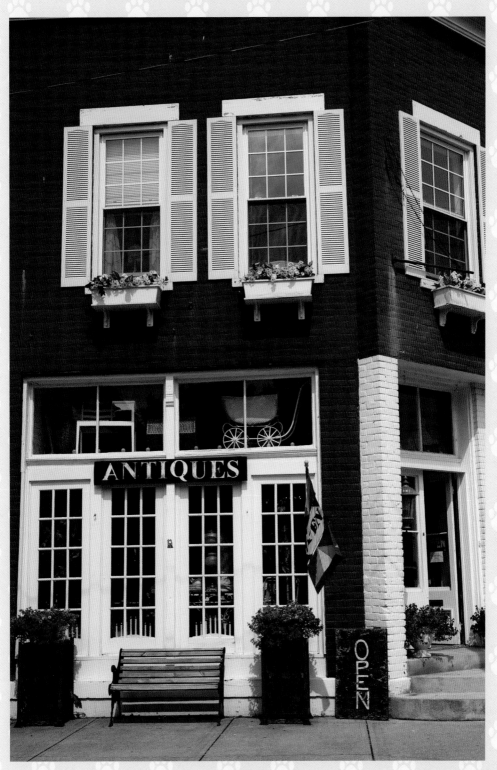

ANTIQUES

OPEN

Answer on page 138.

Answer on page 138.

Answer on page 138.

Answer on page 139.

Answer on page 139.

Answer on page 139.

31

Answer on page 139.

32

33

Answer on page 140.

Answer on page 140.

Answer on page 140.

Answer on page 141.

37

Answer on page 141.

Answer on page 141.

Answer on page 142.

Answer on page 142.

43

Answer on page 142.

Answer on page 143.

45

Answer on page 143.

Answer on page 143.

Answer on page 143.

Answer on page 144.

49

Answer on page 144.

Answer on page 144.

50

51

Answer on page 144.

Answer on page 145.

Answer on page 145.

Answer on page 145.

Answer on page 145.

Answer on page 146.

Answer on page 146.

Answer on page 146.

Answer on page 146.

Answer on page 147.

60

61

Answer on page 147.

Answer on page 147.

Answer on page 147.

Answer on page 148.

Answer on page 148.

Answer on page 148.

Answer on page 149.

69

Answer on page 149.

Answer on page 149.

Answer on page 149.

Answer on page 149.

Answer on page 150.

Answer on page 150.

Answer on page 150.

Answer on page 150.

Answer on page 150.

Answer on page 150.

Answer on page 151.

81

Answer on page 151.

Answer on page 151.

Answer on page 151.

Answer on page 151.

Answer on page 152.

Answer on page 152.

89

Answer on page 152.

Answer on page 152.

Answer on page 152.

Answer on page 153.

Answer on page 153.

Answer on page 153.

Answer on page 153.

Answer on page 153.

Answer on page 153.

Answer on page 154.

Answer on page 154.

Answer on page 154.

101

Answer on page 154.

Answer on page 154.

Answer on page 154.

Answer on page 155.

Answer on page 155.

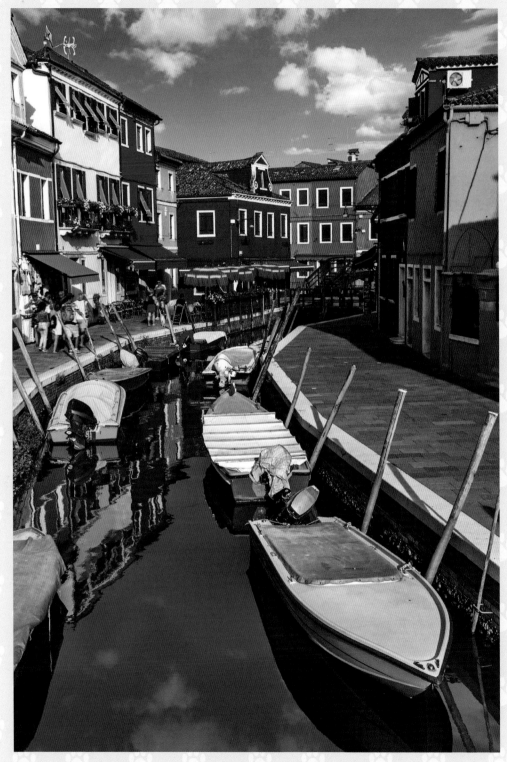

Answer on page 155.

Answer on page 155.

Answer on page 155.

Answer on page 155.

Answer on page 156.

Answer on page 156.

Answer on page 156.

Answer on page 156.

Answer on page 156.

Answer on page 156.

Answer on page 157.

Answer on page 157.

Answer on page 157.

Answer on page 157.

Answer on page 157.

Answer on page 158.

123

Answer on page 158.

Answer on page 158.

Answer on page 159.

127

Answer on page 159.

Answer on page 159.

129

Answer on page 159.

Answer on page 160.

Answer on page 160.

Answer on page 160.

PAGE 4

PAGE 6

PAGE 5

PAGE 7

ANSWERS

PAGE 8

PAGE 10

PAGE 9

PAGE 11

PAGE 12

PAGE 14

PAGE 13

PAGE 15

~ ANSWERS ~

PAGE 16

PAGE 18

PAGE 17

PAGE 19

❧ ANSWERS ❧

PAGE 20

PAGE 22

PAGE 21

PAGE 23

PAGE 24

PAGE 26

PAGE 25

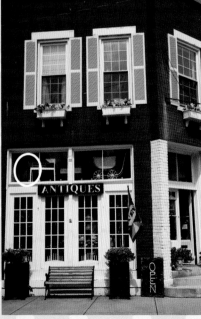

PAGE 27

ANSWERS

PAGE 28

PAGE 30

PAGE 29

PAGE 31

ANSWERS

PAGE 32

PAGE 34

PAGE 33

PAGE 35

ANSWERS

PAGE 36

PAGE 38

PAGE 37

PAGE 39

PAGE 40

PAGE 42

PAGE 41

PAGE 43

PAGE 44

PAGE 46

PAGE 45

PAGE 47

ANSWERS

PAGE 48

PAGE 50

PAGE 49

PAGE 51

144

PAGE 52

PAGE 54

PAGE 53

PAGE 55

PAGE 56

PAGE 58

PAGE 57

PAGE 59

~ ANSWERS ~

PAGE 60

PAGE 62

PAGE 61

PAGE 63

PAGE 64

PAGE 66

PAGE 65

PAGE 67

ANSWERS

PAGE 68

PAGE 70

PAGE 72

PAGE 69

PAGE 71

PAGE 73

ANSWERS

PAGE 74

PAGE 76

PAGE 78

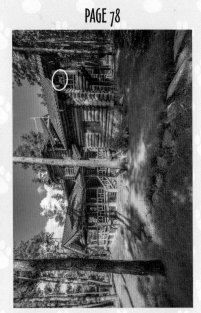

PAGE 75

PAGE 77

PAGE 79

ANSWERS

PAGE 80

PAGE 82

PAGE 84

PAGE 81

PAGE 83

PAGE 85

ANSWERS

PAGE 86

PAGE 88

PAGE 90

PAGE 87

PAGE 89

PAGE 91

PAGE 92

PAGE 94

PAGE 96

PAGE 93

PAGE 95

PAGE 97

PAGE 98

PAGE 100

PAGE 102

PAGE 99

PAGE 101

PAGE 103

ANSWERS

PAGE 104

PAGE 106

PAGE 108

PAGE 105

PAGE 107

PAGE 109

ANSWERS

PAGE 110

PAGE 112

PAGE 114

PAGE 111

PAGE 113

PAGE 115

ANSWERS

PAGE 116

PAGE 118

PAGE 120

PAGE 117

PAGE 119

PAGE 121

~ ANSWERS ~

PAGE 122

PAGE 124

PAGE 123

PAGE 125

ANSWERS

PAGE 126

PAGE 128

PAGE 127

PAGE 129

PAGE 130

PAGE 132

PAGE 131